GW00786306

The Four Great Covenants

By Paul & Nuala O'Higgins

Published & distributed by
Reconciliation Outreach
P.O. Box 2778
Stuart, Florida, USA
34995-2778

AUTHORS' NOTE

This book was previously published under the title "The Four Great Covenants." In this updated and expanded edition we show the biblical reasons why God's covenants are relevant today for the church, Israel and the world.

TABLE OF CONTENTS

INTRODUCTION

WHAT IS A COVENANT?

God's great actions in human history are preceded by His word and His covenants. He speaks then He acts. He makes covenants and He fulfills them. These great contracts or covenants control the history of the world.

God created the world by His word. His word and His actions also accomplish His redemption of the world. God binds Himself to His word and reinforces His commitment to it by entering into contractual relationships with man. These contractual agreements that God made with man were made in the manner of ancient societies - through contracts sealed in blood. These contracts are called covenants.

A covenant is a solemn agreement between two or more persons or groups to do or not to do a certain thing. According to the Bible God has entered into covenant with mankind on several occasions. Since the nature of God is love and truth, He cannot violate His covenant; He cannot fail to do what He has promised. In this way He has made a basis by which we can relate to Him.

Our God is a covenant making, covenant keeping God. Through covenant He has bound Himself to His Word to do what He has promised. When He says He will do something He does it and no power can stop Him. *"For I am the Lord. I speak, and the word which I speak will come to pass"* (Ezek. 12:25)

Those who have entered into covenant with Him have therefore a legal right to call on God to do what He has promised. The relationship between man and God is not governed by *wish* or *hope* but by the *legal* basis of covenant. God in His love has created a covenant with man by which we can approach Him and receive His help.

In primitive societies individuals and tribes frequently entered into covenant with one another. These covenants were sealed in blood. To violate a covenant would result in the penalty of death. By the blood ritual the parties were stating that they were committed even to the point of death to keep their side of the bargain.

The Four Great Covenants

God has entered into a redemptive relationship with mankind through the "covenants of promise" (Ephesians 2:12) Through these He guarantees that He will provide salvation for mankind in spite of our inability to keep our side of the bargain and in spite of our weakness.

God promised the serpent that tempted Adam and Eve: *"I will put enmity between you and the woman and between your seed and her Seed; He shall bruise your head and you shall bruise His heel."* (Genesis 3:15) Here God promised mankind that 'the seed of the woman's seed' would destroy the rule of Satan over their lives. This promise is sometimes called **"The Adamic Covenant".** Later God

11

made a covenant with Noah promising that He would never again destroy the earth with a flood. (Gen. 9:15).

Since this book is focused on the four major Covenants that God made with Israel we are not examining the covenants made with Adam or with Noah.

When God began to execute His plan for the redemption of mankind He called a man, Abram, and entered into covenant with Him and with His descendants. (Gen. 12:1-3,7; Gen. 15; Gen. 17:1-21) About four hundred years later God amplified this covenant at Sinai. There He gave Moses and the descendants of Abraham, Isaac and Jacob instructions for living and worship. (Ex. 19:5; 20:22-23:19) Still later God entered into a further covenant, with David. This covenant with David expands and amplifies Abraham's covenant. (2 Sam. 7:7-16 Psalm 89:3-4, I Chronicles 17:11-14)) Finally He promised a New Covenant, which would deal with the guilt and sin of the people and open up a way for the blessing of Abraham to come in its fullness on the people of Israel and for that blessing to be extended to all nations. (Jeremiah 31:31-34)

In this book we shall focus on the four great covenants of redemption that God made with Abraham and the Children of Israel. These Four Great Covenants are:

(1) The Abrahamic Covenant,
(2) The Mosaic Covenant.
(3) The Davidic Covenant.
(4) The New Covenant.

Each of these covenants involves a solemn entry by God into a contractual arrangement with men to advance His redemptive work on the earth. Each covenant applies to a specific group of people. The benefactor is named, the conditions are listed, and the terms of the covenant are given.

A basic grasp of these covenants is vital to understand

1. God's plan for the world, for Israel and for the Church;
2. the relationship between the Church and Israel,
3. the relationship between law and grace.

CHAPTER 1

THE ABRAHAMIC COVENANT

When God called Abraham and made a covenant with him, He promised to give him and his descendants

(1) an everlasting inheritance -the Land of Canaan

(2) to make his name great

(3) to give him heirs

(4) to bless him

(5) to bless those who bless him and to curse those who curse him, i.e. to judge them by their attitude to Abraham and his descendants. (Genesis 12:1-3)

This covenant was on the basis of God's *call* and *election* and responded to by Abraham's faith.

It was not based on his religious piety. What was required of Abraham was *faith* and *obedience*. He was called to leave *"country, kindred and father's house"* and go to the land of Canaan, where God would bring His promises to pass. It is sometimes stated that this covenant is unconditional. It would be more accurate to say that it was without *moral* conditions, as *faith* and *obedience* were required. (This does not mean that Abraham was exempted from living by the highest ethical standards, but that the Covenant was not made or fulfilled as a *reward* for his moral conduct.) His faith is a model for all subsequent believers.

The Abrahamic Covenant is exclusive to Abraham and His physical descendants through Isaac and Jacob. *"In Isaac shall your seed be called."* (Gen. 21:12) *"The land which I gave Abraham and Isaac I give to you, and to your descendants after you I give this land."* (Genesis 35:12) The *blessings* of this covenant, however are not exclusive to Abraham's descendants but are to spill over on all nations, for God said '*In you all the families of the earth will be blessed."* (Genesis 12:3). This covenant therefore is not merely for the sake of Abraham's descendants but for the sake of all the nations of the world. And so the welfare of all the nations is linked with the fulfillment and recognition of God's call on Abraham and his descendants.

It is an *everlasting* covenant with Abraham's descendants on the basis of God's promises and Abraham's obedience.

- It is not established by the obedience of Abraham's descendants;
- nor is it revoked by their disobedience.

The terms of this covenant are **everlasting**. *'I will establish My covenant between me and you and your descendants after you in their generations, for an everlasting covenant, to be God to you and your descendants after you."* (Gen. 17:7) Because God's covenant with Abraham is everlasting, the *land* of Canaan remains the *everlasting inheritance* of Abraham's descendants through Isaac and Jacob.

"And I will establish My covenant between me and you and your descendants after you in their generation for an everlasting covenant...Also I give to you and your descendants after you the land in which you are a stranger all the land of Canaan, as an everlasting possession." (Gen. 17:7-8)

Though the nations of the world may not recognize this covenant, God remembers it and He will engineer history to see that it is fulfilled. He remembers His covenant and watches over His word to perform it.

When God makes a promise He obligates Himself to bring it to pass. Since God cannot lie . He cannot forget or renege on a promises.

"For I am the Lord. I speak, and the word which I speak will come to pass." (Ezekiel 12.25)

"God is not a man, that He should lie, nor a son of man, that He should repent. Has He said, and will He not do? Or has He spoken, and will He not make it good?" (Number s 23.19)

God fulfilled His promise to Abraham and Sarah in the miraculous birth of a son, Isaac, when she was too old to give birth by the ordinary laws of nature. He fulfilled His word regardless of Abraham's ability, because He had promised in the covenant to give Abraham a son and heir.

Since this covenant still stands today, God will still bless those who honor this covenant. People who respect God's call on the Jewish people will be blessed and those who do not respect it will suffer loss. *"I will bless those who bless you and I will curse him who curses you; and in you all the families of the earth shall be blessed."* (Genesis 12:4)

In the Babylon culture from which Abraham was called, results were produced through natural effort. The people of Babylon – the builders of the Tower Of Babel- were motivated

1. by their own ambitions
2. to produce results for their own glory
3. by means of their own power. (See Genesis 11)

In contrast to this Abraham is called out of this humanistic culture

1. *from* His own ambitions *into* God's plan.
2. to allow God produce results which Abraham is incompetent to produce,
3. by means of God's power,
4. for God's glory.

God promised to extend the blessings of Abraham's Covenant to all the nations through Abraham's seed. *"In you all the nations of the earth shall be blessed, because you have obeyed my voice."* (Gen. 22:18)

The blessing of Abraham is referred to in The Letter to the Galatians (Galatians 3:14). This does not mean that God gives the Gentiles title to the land of promise. If this were the case God would be changing the terms of the everlasting Covenant He made with Abraham and His descendants and making the land the inheritance of all believers. It means that through the Seed of Abraham (the Messiah) the blessing of favor with God will come upon gentiles who turn to God for reconciliation and forgiveness.

Before we move on from our discussion of Abrahamic Covenant, let us restate that it is specifically for his *natural* descendants through Isaac and Jacob. It includes the promise of physical land as a perpetual inheritance, and the promise of a Seed through whom the nations will be blessed.

Since the blessings of Abraham are extended to all believers through Jesus, the walk of Abraham becomes a model for all those who approach God through faith. We cannot really enter into the life of faith without taking the four steps that were required of Abraham

(1) separation from the limitations of family and culture to move with the plan of God,

(2) exchanging our own ambitious for God's plan

(3) looking to God to fulfill His plan by His power,

(4) that God may be glorified.

Today those who recognize the Covenant with Abraham and support God's plans for His descendants will be blessed. In addition each one of us can enter the walk of faith and obedience that he had. Have you embarked on Abraham's walk? Are you honoring the Abrahamic Covenant?

CHAPTER 2

THE SINAI COVENANT

The next Great Covenant through which God discloses His glory to Israel is the Sinai Covenant. God made this covenant with the children of Israel at Mount Sinai when He gave them the Ten Commandments, the code of law and ritual, and the instructions for sacrifices and feasts

This covenant is made between God and the entire children of Israel. (Exodus 19) In this covenant God gives conditions for *enjoying* life in their Promised Land. This covenant delivered by Moses to the Children of Israel at Sinai has two dominant features:

23

(1) a strict code of morality and ritual,

(2) and a system of sacrifices and priesthood. Through these sacrifices failures under the moral and ritual laws were atoned for and fellowship with God's presence was thereby restored.

It is sometimes remarked that the Sinai Covenant, unlike the New Covenant, was a covenant of judgment rather than mercy. This is far from being true. The mercy of God is a dominant part of the Mosaic Covenant. God provided for the atonement of sin and for the continuous access to His grace and mercy through the sacrificial system. This was a central component of the Sinai covenant.

The Blessings & The Curses

Blessings and curses were a dominant feature of the Mosaic Covenant. God promised the Israelis that He would bless them if they faithfully kept the moral and ritual laws of Sinai, but He warned them that if they failed to keep these laws they would forfeit their *enjoyment* of their Promised Land and suffer greatly.

"But it shall come to pass, if you do not obey the

voice of the Lord your God, to observe careful ALL His commandments and His statutes which I command you today, that all these curses will come upon you and overtake you: Cursed shall you be in the city and cursed shall you be in the country. ... The Lord will cause you to be defeated before your enemies.... And you shall be plucked from the land, which you go to possess. Then the Lord will scatter you among all peoples, from one end of the earth to the other.. and among these nations you shall find no rest." (Deuteronomy 28:15,16,25,64,65)

"Now it shall come to pass, when all these things come upon you, ... and you return to the Lord your God and obey His voice according to all that I command you today, you and your children, with all your heart, and with all your soul, that the Lord your God will bring you back from captivity and have compassion on you and gather you again from all the nations where the Lord your God has scattered you...Then the Lord will bring you to the land which your fathers possessed and you shall possess it.... And the Lord your God will circumcise your heart and the heart of your descendants to love the Lord your God with all your heart and with all your soul that you may live." (Deuteronomy 30:1,2,5,6)

God did not threaten to ***cancel*** the Abrahamic Covenant if they failed to keep the

Law of Moses. He warned them that if they did no keep the Sinai Covenant they would ***temporarily*** lose possession of their inheritance and their ***enjoymen****t* of the blessings of Abraham. They would lose their blessing *but not their promise.* They would temporarily lose their enjoyment of their inheritance but would not lose the *promise* of ultimate enjoyment and blessing in the land.

To use a simple example a farmer could through ill health be forced to leave his farm and move to a nursing home. The farm would still be his though he would not be enjoying it. In a similar way Israel, through its repeated failure under the Sinai Covenant, at times forfeited their right to enjoy the land, but not their title deed to it. This is why with every threat of dispersion there is always a promise of eventual restoration.

God wanted the blessing of Abraham to be on a righteous people. Society in Israel was to be a model for the nations, where God would be honored as the center and source of everything. He wanted His ways of loving one another and righteous behavior to be the ruling norm.

The Sinai Covenant adds an element, which

is not seen in Abraham's Covenant - the revelation of sin and human frailty. The Covenant at Sinai reconfirms what God had already revealed to Adam, Eve and Cain - that man is born in sin and sin creates alienation between man and God. Under the Sinai law the children of Israel (in spite of the availability of God's continuous pardon) were constantly confronted with their sin and weakness. The Sinai covenant brought the revelation of sin and the awareness of guilt.

God had given the land of Canaan to Abraham and his descendants forever as an everlasting possession; but in the Sinai Covenant, He made the *enjoyment* of the land conditional on their obedience to the Sinai laws. The consequence of disobedience will be a TEMPORARY forfeiture of the land and the blessings. He warns the Children of Israel that the consequences of their moral failure will be that they will be 'spewn' out of the land. However, He never warns them that they will forfeit their *ownership* of the land, but puts on them strict moral requirements. The land remains their everlasting birthright and they remain His called people forever.

CHAPTER 3

THE NEW COVENANT

The Sinai Covenant with its majestic moral requirements and sacrificial system left the children of Israel and God with two problems.

(1) The Laws of Sinai were an exhortation to righteousness but they were also a guilt-producing reminder of human frailty and sinfulness. The law was powerful to *reveal* human weakness but powerless to *undo* human weakness. Though the daily sacrifices provided atonement and covering for sin, they had no power to *remove* sin.

(2) The second problem, with the Sinai Covenant was that it included, as we have seen, the fearful curses.

The "Yo-Yo" Problem

The curse of the law and the problem of sin create a problem. If God is to fulfill His promise to Abraham then the land of Israel will be the possession of Abraham's descendants forever. However, under the Sinai Law their sinfulness must be punished with exile. We like to call this problem: "God's yo-yo problem."

Under the terms of Abraham's Covenant He is committed to settling His people in their land. Under the Sinai covenant He is forced to drive them out because of their unrighteousness. This creates a historic cycle of scattering and regathering the people of Israel from and to the land.

He settles them in the land; they become disobedient then He must drive them out. Then He recalls them to the land because of His faithfulness to the Abrahamic covenant, but then He must drive them out again because of disobedience. The cycle of return and exile goes on and on, like a yo-yo on a string.

For the Abrahamic Covenant to be permanently fulfilled (i.e. for the children of Israel to live permanently and peacefully in their land) God must solve the problem created by sin and by the curse of the Law. If these problems are not solved then the cycle of gathering and dispersion will go on forever.

The prophets of Israel began to meditate on this problem (We doubt that they called it the "yo-yo" problem!) As they pondered this problem God began to show them what He was about to do. He began to tell them of a coming day when sin would be *permanently* and *fully* atoned for, and the sin nature (or sin principle) taken out of the hearts of the people of Israel.

Isaiah saw God's solution to the problem created by man's sin and *'the curse of the Law.'* He prophesied a coming One who would take on Himself the iniquity of His people. This coming One would become cursed for them and bare on Himself *"the curse of the Law."*

"All we like sheep have gone astray; we have turned every one, to his own way, and the Lord has laid on Him

the iniquity of us all." (Isaiah 53:6) He saw that the cycle of sin, guilt, and temporary loss of inheritance would be broken by the death of the One who would take on Himself the curse of the Law and make permanent atonement for the people.

Jeremiah & Ezekiel prophesy further that the remedy for sin would be provided *not* only through the *obedience of* the Suffering Servant, but by the gift of the Holy Spirit. The Spirit of righteousness would replace the sin principle in man. (Jeremiah 31 & Ezekiel 36)

"For I will take you from among the nations, gather you out of all countries, and bring YOU into your own land Then I will sprinkle clean water on you, and you shall be clean; I will cleanse you from all your filthiness and from all your idols. I will give you a new heart and put a new spirit within you; I will take the heart of stone out of your flesh and give you a heart of flesh. I will put My Spirit within you and cause you to walk in my statutes, and you will keep my judgments and *do them. Then you shall dwell* in *the land that I gave to your fathers; you shall be My people, and I will be Your God."* (Ezekiel 36:24-28)

"Behold the days are coming says the Lord, when I will make **a new covenant** *with the house of Israel and the house of Judah... I will put my law in their minds and write it on their hearts; and I will be their God and they shall be My people."* (Jer. 31:31 & 33)

The New Covenant overcomes the problem of sin by the impartation of a new heart and a new Spirit. The heart of stone - the sinful selfish side of our nature - which is common to all the sons of Adam (Jew and Gentile alike), is replaced with a heart of flesh – a soft unselfish heart- through the gift of the Holy Spirit. The repeated sacrifices (repeated daily because they were made with temporal and finite animals) are replaced by the eternal sacrifice of Jesus.

With the New Covenant the righteous standards of God are not just written on tablets of stone but written on the hearts and minds of the believers. Righteousness is no longer a merely external standard but an inner life which God will place in the hearts of His people, Since the essence of the Law is summed up in the two great commandments *"You shall love the Lord your God with all your heart, with all your soul, and with all your strength." (Deut. 6.5) "you shall love your neighbor as yourself."* (Lev. 19.18)

Moses prophecies: *"The Lord God will raise up a prophet after Me, him you must listen to"* (Deut. 18:15) This is a prophecy of a greater mediator than Moses, who would take the people of Israel further than Moses has taken them.

John the Baptist brings Isaiah's prophecy of a Suffering Servant and the prophecies of Ezekiel and Jeremiah together when He announces Jesus as the "Lamb of God" and the one who would baptize with the Holy Spirit. *"The next day John saw Jesus coming toward him, and said, 'Behold! The Lamb of God who takes away the sin of the world! I did not know Him, but He who sent me to baptize with water said to me: 'Upon whom you see the Spirit descending, and remaining on Him, this is He who baptizes with the Holy Spirit."* (John 1:29 & 33)

The New Covenant then surpasses the Sinai Covenant because it solves the problem of the curse of the Law and provides a means for implanting righteousness in the hearts of believers. It does not *replace* the Sinai Covenant; it *fulfills* it.

The New Covenant provides permanent atonement, and redeems us from the curse of the law. Paul says: *"The Messiah has redeemed us from the curse of the law having become a curse for us."* (Gal. 3:12)

Moses gave the people of God commandments on tablets of stone, but by implanting the Spirit of God who is love in the hearts of the believers, Jesus fills hearts with God's love and nature and makes them people who know and love God and forgive and love their neighbor in the power of a new nature.

The penalty of the curse is twofold:
- forfeiture of the land *and*
- forfeiture of blessing.

Isaiah foretold the Messiah would take these curses on Himself so that the curse could be lifted, from the children of Israel. This now makes it possible for God to fulfill the Abrahamic Covenant without further dispersion of the Jewish people - provided they accept God's offer.

Our Heavenly Father, who so loved the world, sent His Son to be the perfect Lamb to fulfill, once for all, the type and shadow of the

Passover Lamb, not only the for the descendants of Abraham but for all mankind When the time came for Jesus' final Passover, He said, *"Father, not my will but thine be done,"* and became that perfect Lamb. He declared to them, *"This is My blood of the NEW COVENANT, which is shed for* **many***."* (Mark 14.24). By this gentiles are included.

The New Covenant is more than God's solution to the yo-yo problem' for Abraham's descendants. This covenant also means that when Yeshua died as the perfect Lamb, He took to the Cross the source of sin and rebellion - the SIN of the world - i.e. the Adam man and Adam nature. He gives us in exchange His own Spirit and nature - what a deal! His Cross fulfills all the other sacrifices including the Tempe sacrifices for every kind of sin.

We, Jews and gentiles alike, have only to believe, receive and live by the power of this NEW LIFE made available through His resurrection.

The Sinai Covenant laws are preceded by the words "You shall" or "You shall not."

The New Covenant is preceded with the words "I (God) will take out the heart of stone" and "I (God) will put my spirit within them." It is God's achievement for us and gift to us.

CHAPTER 4

THE NEW COVENANT
& THE SINAI COVENANT

The New Covenant fulfills the Sinai Covenant in three ways

1) The Temple sacrifices are fulfilled by the eternal sacrifice of Jesus, Lamb of God.(Hebrews Chapters 8-10)

2) The righteousness that the laws of Sinai pointed to is fulfilled when the Spirit of righteousness is imparted into the hearts of those, who admitting the bankruptcy of their self-righteousness, put their trust in the Lamb of God.

3) When the Spirit infilled believer responds to the love God places in his heart, devotes himself

to loving God and his fellow man and lives in harmony with the teachings of Jesus, he fulfills the righteousness that Sinai pointed to. All the moral laws of Sinai could be summed up in the two commandments to love the Lord God with all our hearts and to love our neighbor as ourselves. *'A lawyer, asked him (Jesus) a question to test him. "Teacher, which is the great commandment in the Law?" And he said to him, "You shall love the Lord your God with all your heart and with all your soul and with all your mind. This is the great and first commandment. And a second is like it: You shall love your neighbor as yourself. On these two commandments depend all the Law and the Prophets."'* (Matthew 22: 35-40)

The New Covenant provides *permanent* atonement for all transgressions of the Sinai Law and places a spirit of love in our hearts that empowers us to love God and others. It thus fulfills the Sinai Covenant. Since permanent atonement is provided we are discharged from the curse of the law and free to serve the Lord by the power of the Spirit.

We are not discharged from the *righteousness* of the law but we are *made righteous* so that we can live righteously. The law was a restraint on our unrighteous nature. The New Covenant gives us a new nature by which we serve God by yielding to His Spirit.

As long as we are unrighteous and behaving unrighteously we are in need of the Sinai Law. When we are righteous and living righteously we do not need the Law to warn us. As Paul puts it: *"The law was our tutor to bring us to Messiah, that we might be justified by faith But after faith has come we are no longer under a tutor."* (Gal 3:24-25) The Sinai Law is not removed. When we come into Christ and live by His righteousness - we are removed from *it*.

The Transition From Sinai Obedience To New Covenant Obedience

The event of the Transfiguration marks the transition that the Jewish disciples of Jesus were to make from following Moses and the Prophets to following Jesus. When Peter wanted to make three tabernacles, one for Moses, one for Elijah and one for Jesus, the voice of the Father was heard saying: *"'This is my beloved Son, in whom I am well pleased Hear*

Him!'.. *When they had lifted up their eyes they saw no one but Jesus* only." (Mt. 17:5 & 8) Moses' and Elijah's glory was fading in the presence of Jesus.

Paul says that those who go 'back under the law' make Christ of no avail, and that the law was our tutor until Jesus came. *"The law was our tutor to bring us to Messiah, that we might be justified by faith But after faith has come we are no longer under a tutor."* (Gal 3:24-25) Paul is very strong in asserting the importance of moving from obedience to the Law to obedience to the Messiah. *'You have become estranged from Christ, you who would attempt to be justified by the law, - you have fallen from grace."* (Gal 4:4) In Philippians he says that he has no righteousness based on law but that which is through faith. (Phil. 3:9)

Paul teaches that, though the law has not been done away with, we have become "dead to the law" through our imputed co-death with Jesus so that we can now come under the control of the Spirit of God. (Romans 6 & 7) Release from the law is not a license to Sin but operates only as we "reckon ourselves dead" to sin (Romans 6:11) *and* yield ourselves as "slaves of righteousness"

(Romans 6:16) by coming under the control of the Holy Spirit. Under the Law the Jewish people have failed to attain righteousness but now in the Messiah righteousness is being offered to them as a *free gift* apart from and in spite of their failure to keep the law.

In Hebrews he says that when there is a change of the priesthood *"of necessity there is also a change of the law...* (Heb. 7:12) The priesthood of the law with its repeated sacrifices was a foretaste of the eternal priesthood that would not require repeated sacrifices. The sacrifices at the Temple have been fulfilled by the eternal sacrifice of Jesus. (If the Temple is rebuilt in the future. it will not be to restore animal sacrifices but to serve as a *"House of prayer for all the peoples"* (Mt. 21:13)

The priesthood is changed and so we come under a different law. There is no lawlessness or anti-nomianism involved here. In Jesus we are not left without law but we are brought from one law to another, i.e. from the law of commandment and ordinances to the law of the Spirit of Life and to the New Commandment. *"A new commandment I give to you that you love one another as I have loved you, that you*

41

also love one another. " (John 13:34)

Becoming Obsolete

The Book of Hebrews tells us the old law is 'becoming obsolete" (Hebrews 8:13) and Jesus tells us that *"the Law and the prophets were UNTIL John, since then the Kingdom of God has been preached and everyone is pressing into it."* (Luke 16:16)

He does not say that it *is* obsolete but that it *is becoming* obsolete. Why does he say that the first law is *becoming* obsolete? Why does he not say simply say that the first Law *is* obsolete? Because the law is not changed, altered or destroyed. It remains the same. It is our *relationship* to it that changes. The law is not removed. It becomes obsolete in our lives as we

- put our faith in the fact that our sins have been eternally atoned for by the eternal sacrifice of Jesus on the cross,
- and in the fact the sin principle in us (the old man) has been crucified with the Messiah. Sin no longer controls us when we give ourselves to be controlled by the Spirit of

God instead of the selfish Adam nature.

The Law (not in the sense of the Torah or the Tanach but in the sense of the regulations of Sinai) is becoming obsolete as people enter into the realm of the Kingdom of God, come under the Lordship of Messiah, and yield to the control of His Spirit. The law *restrains* the sin principle in man. When the sin principle is *replaced* it no longer needs to be *restrained*.

New Testament faith consists not in *restraining* the sin principle by religious laws but in *replacing* it by the life of the Spirit. The believer does not *restrain* the sin principle within him; instead he sees that sin principle dead in Christ and refuses to respond to it. (Romans 6:6 & 6:11)

New Covenant's Ultimate Fulfillment

Since the call of Abraham none of God's covenants of redemption have been made primarily with the Gentiles. The New Covenant also was not made primarily with the Gentiles but with the House of Israel and the House of Judah.

God spoke through Jeremiah that He would make a 'new covenant' with the House of Israel and with the House of Judah (Jer. 31:31) and Jesus declared that His blood inaugurates this New Covenant (Mt. 26:28)

Jesus' death on the cross atones not only for the sins of the House of Israel and the House of Judah but also for the sins of the whole world. (Isaiah tells us that the Lord laid on him *"the iniquity of us all."* He also prophesies that the Messiah would be "a light to the Gentiles" (Isaiah 49:6) and bring *"righteousness to the Gentiles"* (Isaiah 42:1) Furthermore Jesus Himself tells us that He was to be lifted up *"as Moses lifted up the brazen serpent in the wilderness."* This would extend God's redemption to the whole world that *"**whoever** believes in Him should not perish but have everlasting life.'* (John 3:14-16)

Though the New Covenant is made with the Jews its blessings of reconciliation with God are made available to *all men. "God was in Messiah reconciling the world to Himself"* (2 Cor. 5:19). John says: *"as many as received Him to them He gave the right to become children of God."* (John 1:12)

The blessings of reconciliation, redemption, and emancipation from the power of sin are made available to as many Jews or Gentiles that believe in Him and put their faith in His once for all sacrifice.

The New Covenant Is Jewish Too

Some say that the Sinai Covenant is for the Jews and the New Covenant is for the Gentiles. The scriptures say, however, that the New Covenant is also for the Jews. The Gentiles get in on the blessings, partly as a result of Jewish recalcitrance (see Romans 11) and partly to fulfill the promise made to Abraham. The New Covenant is not the Gentiles' Covenant but God's greatest covenant with the Jewish people in which the Gentiles are included.

"Behold the days are coming when I will make a New Covenant with the House of Israel and the House of Judah." (Jer. 31) Here Jeremiah clearly shows that the New Covenant is primarily addressed to the children of Israel. Jesus however when He inaugurated the New Covenant said, *"this is My blood of the new covenant which is shed for many for the*

remission of sins." (Mt. 24:28) He extends the blessings of the New Covenant beyond the House of Israel and Judah to all believers. This fulfills the promise made to Abraham that through His seed all nations would be blessed. (Gen. 12:4)

Provoking Jewish People To Jealousy

Paul writes*; "salvation has come to the Gentiles to provoke the Jewish people to jealousy."* (Romans 11:11) How can this happen? They will be provoked to jealousy *not* by Gentiles being envious of what Jews have, but by the Jews becoming jealous of what the Gentile believers have received. We ought to provoke them to jealousy because the Covenant, that is blessing and redeeming us, is a covenant that belongs to them. Its blessings are only extended to us through overflow.

To provoke them to jealousy the Church should clearly show the Jewish people:

(1) that we understand that the Abrahamic Covenant promises and blessings are not revoked and we recognize that God has given them the Land of Israel;

(2)   that we understand the New Covenant is primarily addressed to them;

(3)   that we renounce, repent and make reparation for any replacement theology and its consequences;

(4) that through the power of the Holy Spirit we live the love commandment;

(5) that we seek to receive all the blessings God has made available to us, and to bring the blessings of redemption to the nations.

Scripture tells us that *"Jews request a sign, and Greeks seek after wisdom."*(I Cor. 1:22) These signs are not road signs or banners but the signs of being blessed, anointed with the Spirit of God and experiencing the miraculous works of God today. The holiness and selfless love that the Holy Spirit can inspire manifests the presence of God today and can provoke our beloved Jewish people to jealousy.

CHAPTER 5

THE ONE NEW MAN

The New Covenant brings Jews and gentiles together.

"Therefore remember that you, once Gentiles in the flesh - who are called uncircumcision by what is called the circumcision made in the flesh by hands - that at that time you were without Messiah being aliens from the commonwealth of Israel and strangers from the covenants of promise, having no hope and without God in the world. But now in Messiah Jesus, you who once were far off have been brought near by the blood of Messiah. For He Himself is our peace, who has made both one, and has broken down the middle wall of separation, having abolished in His flesh, the enmity, that is the law of commandments contained in

ordinances, so as to create in Himself **one new man**
from the two thus making peace" (Ephesians 2:11-15)

By uniting believers with Himself through
the Blood of Jesus and through the gift of the Holy
Spirit, God brings forth a "new creation" on the
earth. This new creation consists of those who
have accepted the gift of the Holy Spirit. These
believers have been brought into intimacy with
God through the Blood of Jesus and cleansed of all
their unrighteousness.

In this realm there is *"neither Jew nor Greek,
there is neither slave nor free, there is neither male nor female,
for you are all one in Messiah Jesus."* (Gal 3:28) All who
put their faith in Jesus have been equally accepted
and adopted into His family. With respect to *call*
and *function* differences still remain, obviously,
between Jew and Greek, male and female, but in
the realm of *acceptance by God,* and being made
partakers of His glory there is *no* distinction.

Those who have received the new life of the
Holy Spirit form *One New Man*, a body of people
dispersed among the nations to show forth the

glory and love of God, and be ambassadors for the Messiah.

When Jews and Gentiles put their faith in the blood of Jesus they are reconciled to God and become partners together with God. The enmity between them is gone and they begin to work together for God's purposes. The Gentile no longer lives as a Gentile, hostile to God's purposes, but lives in solidarity with God's purposes. The Jew is no longer separated from God or from the Gentiles by the guilt produced by the ordinances of the Law. Together they both serve the Lord.

This does not mean that the Jew stops being a Jew or the Gentile become a Jew, *they become one in the Spirit of God*, in the blessing of God, and in the purposes of God, but retain different calls.

Believers from the nations who ignore God's ancient covenant people are acting as if the dividing wall were still up. Though Jewish believers and Gentile believers may adopt different styles of worship to relate to their different cultures, there is not a Jewish Church and a Gentile Church. There is *one Body* and one

Church. Within that Church, Jew and Gentile are one.

The New Covenant reconciles Jew and Gentile with one another and with God. Jew and Gentile become one not at Sinai, nor by the adoption of Jewish religious practices but by faith in the Blood of Jesus and being filled with His Spirit of love. Anti-Semitism shows disrespect for God's covenants, and violates the love commandment. An anti-Semitic Christian is a contradiction and a travesty.

CHAPTER 6

THE DAVIDIC COVENANT

The fourth major covenant God made with Israel is the covenant He made with King David to establish his dynasty *forever*. This is known as *"The Davidic Covenant."* This covenant introduces elements of God's plan that we do not see in the other covenants. It reveals His plan to bring a golden age to Israel and to the entire world which Jesus calls *"The Kingdom Of God."*

Towards the end of David's life (ca. 970 B.C.) God spoke to Nathan, the prophet in a vision. In this vision God gave him a message for

King David, promising that one of David's descendants would inherit his throne and that his kingdom would endure forever.

"When your days are fulfilled
and you lie down with your fathers,
I will raise up your offspring after you,
who shall come forth from your body,
and I will establish his kingdom.
He shall build a house for my name,
and I will establish the throne of his kingdom **forever**.
I will be his Father, and he shall be my son...
And your house and your kingdom shall be made sure
forever before me, your throne shall be established
forever.*"* (2 Sam 7:12-14,16)

"And it shall be, when your days are fulfilled, when you must go to be with your fathers, that I will set up your seed after you, who will be of your sons; and I will establish his kingdom. He shall build Me a house, and I will establish his throne forever. I will be his Father, and he shall be My son; and I will not take My mercy away from him, as I took it from him who was before you.. And I will establish him in My house and in My kingdom forever; and his throne shall be established **forever**.*"* (1 Chron. 17:11-14)

In Psalm 89 this promise is repeated and is described as a covenant.

"I have exalted one chosen from the people
I have found my servant David;
with my holy oil I have anointed him, with whom My
hand shall be established...
My faithfulness and My Mercy shall be with him....
Also I will make him My first born,
the highest of the kings of the earth.
My mercy I will keep for him **forever***,*
And My COVENANT shall stand firm with
His seed also I will make to endure forever, and his throne
as the days of heaven...
Once I have sworn by My holiness;
I will not lie to David
His seed shall endure **forever***,*
And his throne as the sun before Me."
(Psalm 89:20-21; 24-29; 35-37)

These prophetic words are repeated and amplified in several of the Psalms and in the writings of Ezekiel, Jeremiah, Zechariah and Isaiah.

"Surely I will take the children of Israel from
among the nations, wherever they have gone, and will gather
them from every side and bring them into their own

land; and I will make them one nation in the land, on the mountains of Israel; **and one king shall be king over them all**; .....

"David My servant shall be king over them, and they shall all have one shepherd; ..... **and My servant David shall be their prince forever.**

(Ezekiel 37:21-23; 24-25)

Elements Of The Davidic Covenant

We can see from these two passages that there are four main elements to the Davidic Covenant:

(1) The restoration of the throne of David.
(2) The promise that one specific descendant of David will be the permanent occupant of the throne of David.
(3) Jerusalem will be the center of His rule.
(4) The anointed king will be "the highest of the kings of the earth".

(1) The Restoration Of The Throne Of David

Through this covenant, God formally

promises and guarantees to restore the Throne of David, and makes a solemn promise with David that his throne would endure forever..

Though the prophets foresaw and foretold the ***collapse*** of the House of David, they also foresaw its ***restoration***. This Covenant guarantees its restoration. Just as the Covenant with Abraham guarantees the restoration of ***the people*** of Israel to their land, the Covenant with David guarantees the restoration of ***the house and throne*** of David.

In one sentence Jeremiah simultaneously foretold the scattering and regathering of Israel:

"Hear the word of the LORD, O nations,
And declare it in the isles afar off, and say,
'He who scattered Israel will gather him,
And keep him as a shepherd does his flock.' (Jer. 31.10)

Similarly in two brief sentences Ezekiel foretells the overthrow and reestablishment of the throne of David.

"Thus says the Lord God:
"Remove the turban, and take off the crown;
Nothing shall remain the same.
Exalt the humble, and humble the exalted.
Overthrown, overthrown, I will make it overthrown! It

> *shall be no longer,*
> *Until He comes whose right it is,*
> *And I will give it to Him."* (Ezekiel 21:26-27)

The last descendant of David to sit on the throne of David in Jerusalem was Zedekiah. He was deposed from office in the year 586 BC. by the Babylonians. The rule of the House of David over Judah came to an end and has never been restored. BUT IT WILL BE!

(2) One Specific Descendant Of David Will Be The Permanent Occupant Of The Throne Of David

In the Davidic Covenant, David is promised that one specific son will be his heir and will become the highest of the Kings of the earth. This anointed son of David is referred to as "The Messiah" – "The Anointed One"

And My COVENANT shall stand firm with His seed also I will make to endure forever, and his throne as the days of heaven... (Psalm 89.24)

In this verse we are told that not only will the *throne* of David's greater son endure forever, but *one particular king* will reign on it forever. The

Messiah King will reign over the house of David forever.

The promise of one particular anointed king (Messiah) becoming the permanent King of Israel, was repeated and reinforced by the Angel Gabriel who visited Mary of Nazareth. She was promised that she was to conceive a son who would *"reign over the house of Jacob forever."*

"Behold, you will conceive in your womb and bring forth a Son, and shall call His name JESUS. He will be great, and will be called the Son of the Highest; and the Lord God will give Him the throne of His father David. And He will reign over the house of Jacob forever, and of His kingdom there will be no end." (Luke 1:31-34)

According to the prophecies and promises that make up the Davidic Covenant one singular leader will restore the Throne of David. Furthermore he will reign over the house of Jacob forever and his kingdom will never end.

Solomon, David's son and first successor, achieved greatness but did not fulfill the promise of reigning over the house of David forever. His reign was a mere forty years.

Later prophets, prophesying long after the death of Solomon, gave further descriptions of identity of The Messiah King.

1. Micah foretold that he would be born in Bethlehem. (Micah 5.2)

2. Zechariah foretold that the Messiah would at first not be recognized by his own people. He would be "pierced by the inhabitants of Jerusalem before they would later be recognized by him. (Zechariah 11:4-14, 12:10

3. <u>David foretold that after his death the Anointed One would be buried but would not decay in the grave.</u> For you will not abandon my soul to Sheol, or let your holy one see corruption. (Psalm 16.10)

4. Isaiah says the gentiles will trust in Him and before he reigns on the throne of David, he will be *"despised and rejected"* (Isaiah 53.3)

There is only one person in history who fits these descriptions – Yeshua of Nazareth. He was announced as the Son of David,. He was born in Bethlehem "pierced", crucified and killed in Jerusalem, buried but resurrected before his body knew corruption as David prophesied (Psalm

16.10). He is alive forevermore and has promised to return to take the throne of David.

(3) Jerusalem Will Be The Center Of The Messiah's Rule.

The scriptures are not silent about *the location of the future throne of David* – it is Jerusalem. The place from which the Messiah will rule is Jerusalem. It will not be in London, (the location of the greatest present day monarchy), Rome (the location of the largest centralized church authority), New York (the greatest center of international rule and banking) or any other place other than the place promised by God Himself.

"For the LORD HAS CHOSEN
ZION(JERUSALEM) ;
He has desired it for His dwelling place:
"This is My resting place forever;
Here I will dwell, for I have desired it.
I will abundantly bless her [e]provision;
I will satisfy her poor with bread.
I will also clothe her priests with salvation,
And her saints shall shout aloud for joy.
There I will make the horn of David grow;

I will prepare a lamp for My Anointed.
His enemies I will clothe with shame,
But upon Himself His crown shall flourish. " (Ps 132: 13-18)
"Thus says the LORD: 'I will return to Zion,
And dwell in the midst of Jerusalem.
Jerusalem shall be called the City of Truth,
The Mountain of the LORD of hosts,
The Holy Mountain.'" (Zechariah 8.3)

This was the faith and hope of the first followers and apostles of Jesus. They had witnessed Him inaugurate and seal the New Covenant through His death and resurrection but they had one major question to ask Him before He ascended to His throne in heaven. *""Lord, will You at this time restore the kingdom to Israel?"* (Acts 1.6)

Jesus did not directly answer their question but told them that it was not for them know the times fixed by His Father. They were to set their hearts and minds on receiving the Holy Spirit who would give them ability to proclaim the reconciliation accomplished in the New Covenant to the ends of the earth. However, as they watched Him ascend into heaven two angels spoke to them saying: *"This same Jesus, who was taken up from you into heaven, will so come in like manner as you saw Him go into heaven."*

This was the answer to their question about restoring the Kingdom to Israel. Yes Jesus will return and this will be to claim the throne of David and restore the Kingdom of Israel and reign from Jerusalem.

Zechariah also supports these words in predicting that the Messiah will inaugurate his rule by coming to the Mount of Olives in great power and authority.

"Then the Lord will go forth
And fight against those nations,
As He fights in the day of battle.
And in that day His feet will stand on the Mount of Olives,
Which faces Jerusalem on the east.
Thus the Lord my God will come,
And all the saints with [c]You.
And the Lord shall be King over all the earth.
In that day it shall be—
"The Lord is one,"
And His name one." (Zechariah 8:3-4; 8-9)

(4) The Rule Of The Messiah Will Be World Wide

The Davidic Covenant promises that the rule of the Messiah will be centered in Jerusalem as we have seen but it will also extend to the whole earth. This introduces a whole new scale to the rule of the Messiah. The Davidic Covenant promises not just a golden age of peace and prosperity for Israel - it also promises a golden age for all nations. The failed and corrupt systems of human government will be replaced by the incorruptible rule of the Messiah.

According to the covenant promises God says that David's greater Son – the Messiah – will be "the highest of the kings of the earth."

Also I will make him My firstborn,
the highest of the kings of the earth.
My mercy I will keep for him forever. (Psalm 89:24-25

Zechariah amplifies this covenant promise when he proclaims that the Messiah will not only be the greatest king on the earth but will rule over the entire earth.

"And the Lord shall be King over all the earth. In that day

it shall be "The Lord is one," and His name one." (Zech. 14.9)

Though the rule of David was limited to the land of Israel, the restored kingdom will be a kingdom over the entire world. The fact that the Messiah will rule over all nations is also clearly stated in Daniel.

> *"I was watching in the night visions,*
> *And behold, One like the Son of Man,*
> *Coming with the clouds of heaven!*
> *He came to the Ancient of Days,*
> *And they brought Him near before Him.*
> *Then to Him was given dominion and glory and a*
> *kingdom,*
> *That all peoples, nations, and languages should serve*
> *Him.*
> *His dominion is an everlasting dominion,*
> *Which shall not pass away,*
> *And His kingdom the one*
> *Which shall not be destroyed.* (Daniel 7:13-14)

The Messiah's kingdom will replace every other rule and authority. It will be a kingdom in complete harmony with God's ways, God's mercy and God's will. It will extend all nations and replace every other rule and authority.

As John sees it: *"And the seventh angel sounded, and there were great voices in Heaven, saying, "The kingdoms of this world are become the kingdoms of our Lord and of His Christ, and He shall reign for ever and ever!"* (Revelation 11.15)

The enthronement of the Messiah as the king over all the kingdoms of this world is the climax and goal of history. The words of the prophets show that God is engineering world history to a glorious conclusion. He has a wonderful plan to unite heaven and earth together under the rule of the Messiah.

"For he has made known to us in all wisdom and insight the mystery of his will, according to his purpose which he set forth in Christ (The Messiah King) as a plan for the fulness of time, to unite all things in him, things in heaven and things on earth." (Ephesians 1:9-10)

The fulfillment of the Davidic Covenant and the establishment of his throne in Jerusalem will inaugurate this Golden age. The long era of man's mismanagement of the earth come to an end. The earth will be delivered from its bondage to strife between nations and social injustice, spiritual darkness and oppression.

Isaiah emphasizes this aspect of the Messiah's rule.

"Now it shall come to pass in the latter days
That the mountain of the Lord's house
Shall be established on the top of the mountains,
And shall be exalted above the hills;
And all nations shall flow to it.
Many people shall come and say,
"Come, and let us go up to the mountain of the LORD,
To the house of the God of Jacob;
He will teach us His ways,
And we shall walk in His paths. "
For out of Zion shall go forth the law,
And the word of the LORD from Jerusalem.
He shall judge between the nations,
And rebuke many people;
They shall beat their swords into plowshares,
And their spears into pruning [a]hooks;
Nation shall not lift up sword against nation,
Neither shall they learn war anymore." (Isaiah 2:2-4)

This will be a golden age for all the earth.

The return of the Messiah is not simply the enthronement of a new righteous leader and king over Israel. It has much wider implications. It foretells a golden age over the entire of world when the blessings of Abraham will be enjoyed by Israel and all the nations under the benign rule of the Messiah.

This is what the New Testament calls "the Kingdom of God". God will rule over the earth through His Son and curse and remove every rule and authority hostile to His rule of love and life. This includes the replacement of visible and invisible kingdoms and powers that are opposed the blessed and kindly rule of God. The failed systems of human rule will be replaced by the incorruptible rule of God through His incorruptible Son. The devil and his minions that brought corruption and bondage on the descendants of Adam will be bound and his influence removed.

This will be the consummation of the prayer that Yeshua gave His disciples to pray: *"Thy Kingdom come on earth as it is in heaven."* The Messiah will return and will reign over all the earth. The devil will be bound and removed. Weapons of war will be turned into weapons of productivity. Ideologies of hate, oppression and strife will be replaced and each one will learn to walk in the ways of love and kindness.

When Will The Davidic Covenant Be Fulfilled?

The question still arises when will the Messiah restore the throne of David and establish his rule over Israel and the nations?

Jews can be understood for not recognizing Yeshua as the Messiah, because when he came the first time he did not restore the throne of David nor rid Israel of its enemies. Instead His coming was followed by a time of destruction and humiliation of Israel. The question for Israel is when will the Messiah come to rule in victory from Jerusalem; and the question for Christians is when will Jesus (who we know to be the Messiah) come and rule over Israel and the world?

Believers of every generation have

anticipated the restoration of the throne of David and the open rule of the Messiah from Jerusalem. They often inquire when this great event will take place.

The disciples asked Jesus *"What is the sign of your coming and of the end of the age?"* (Matt. 24.2) They wanted to know when He was coming to take the throne of David and overthrow the enemies of Israel. He answered by foretelling the fall of the Temple and of Jerusalem. He concludes by foretelling the regathering and the restoration of Jerusalem once again to Jewish control.

"Jerusalem will be trampled down underfoot by the gentiles UNTIL the times of the gentiles is fulfilled." (Luke 21.24) *"Times of the gentiles"* means the time of gentile domination over Jerusalem. Jesus' answer to the question, *"What will be the sign of your coming?"* is that it will come after the scattering and regathering of Israel when gentile dominion over Jerusalem comes to an end. Gentile dominion over Jerusalem came to an end in 1967. His coming to take the throne of David will come soon after the restoration of Israel and Jerusalem.

This agrees with the prophetic word of Ezekiel spoken 500 years before Jesus.

"Thus says the Lord God: "Surely I will take the children of Israel from among the nations, wherever they have gone, and will gather them from every side and bring them into their own land;

and I will make them one nation in the land, on the mountains of Israel;

and one king shall be king over them all; *they shall no longer be two nations, nor shall they ever be divided into two kingdoms again ... .*

"David My servant shall be king over them, and they shall all have one shepherd; *they shall also walk in My judgments and observe My statutes, and do them. Then they shall dwell in the land that I have given to Jacob My servant, where your fathers dwelt; and they shall dwell there, they, their children, and their children's children, forever;* **and My servant David shall be their prince forever.** ' "* (Ezek. 37:21-22; 24-25)

Here we can clearly see the restoration of the Davidic Kingdom and the enthronement of the Messiah as King of Judah comes after the restoration of the Jewish people from all the nations where they were scattered. It is evident that the present day restoration of Israel is an exact fulfillment of these prophecies of Ezekiel, Jeramiah and Jesus and all the other prophets who foretold Israel's restoration.

This restoration of the throne of David is identical to the return of Yeshua. He came first to inaugurate the New Covenant through His death and resurrection and is coming again to take the throne of David.

The time line, that the throne of David will be reestablished when Israel comes back from its exile among the nations, is reinforced by prophetic words of Jeremiah:

"Thus says the Lord:
'Again there shall be heard in this place - of which you
say, "It is desolate, without man and without beast"- in
the cities of Judah, in the streets of Jerusalem that are
desolate, without man and without inhabitant and without
beast, the voice of joy and the voice of gladness, the voice of
the bridegroom and the voice of the bride, the voice of those
who will say: of him who counts them,' says the Lord.
'In those days and at that time I will cause to grow up to
David - a Branch of righteousness;
He shall execute judgment and righteousness in the earth.

In those days Judah will be saved,
And Jerusalem will dwell safely....
"For thus says the Lord: 'David shall never lack a man to
sit on the throne of the house of Israel.'"
(Jeremiah 33:10,11,15-17)

The prophets Ezekiel, Jeremiah and Yeshua are in perfect harmony in predicting the establishment of the throne of David after Israel's exile to the nations and the desolation of Jerusalem come to an end.

Because we are living in these days of restoration it is fitting that we should set our hearts and hopes on the coming of the Messiah to restore the throne of David and inaugurate the golden age of righteousness and peace for Israel and the entire world. Like the wise virgins in Jesus parable our hearts should be filled with eager anticipating of these great events which are being activated from heaven on the earth and this amazing juncture of history.

The Davidic Covenant & Jerusalem

It is clear that if the world wide rule of the

Messiah is to be established He must replace and remove every other rule and authority. This is what is described in the images of the Book of Revelation. Here the struggle to replace Babylon with the New Jerusalem is depicted. (Babylon represents the systems of human independent government, with its governmental and banking systems making decisions based on humanistic principles without reference to God.) The systems that presently prevail over the whole earth will be replaced.

The establishment and fulfillment of the Davidic Covenant calls for the overthrow of Babylon. This is why in Revelation 21 the coming of the Lord is presented as the overthrow of Babylon and celebration goes up among the angels and saints.

"After these things I saw another angel coming down from heaven, having great authority, and the earth was illuminated with his glory. And he cried mightily with a loud voice, saying, "Babylon the great is fallen, is fallen, and has become a dwelling place of demons, a prison for every foul spirit, and a cage for every unclean and hated bird! [3] *For all the nations have drunk of the wine of the*

wrath of her fornication, the kings of the earth have committed fornication with her, and the merchants of the earth have become rich through the abundance of her luxury." (Revelations 18.1-3)

Indeed the fall of Babylon is celebrated six times in the book of Revelation (Revelation 14.8; 16:19; 17;5: 18:2: 18:10: 18:21.

We know from the prophets and from Paul that the present ruling systems are heavily influenced and dominated by unseen demonic forces and spirits which Paul call the *"rulers of this present darkness and wicked spirits in the heavenlies"* (Ephesians 6.12.) Therefore to establish Messiah's throne in Jerusalem and over the whole world requires the removal of the rebellious spirits that oppress humanity directly and through ruling governmental systems of this age.

It Will Surely Happen!

God's word tells us that this will happen, and the word which He speaks He brings to pass (Ezekiel 12.25). David's Son will sit on the throne of Israel. According to the prophets this promise would be fulfilled by one who was to be born in

Bethlehem (Micah 5:2) and who would be called "Mighty God." (Isaiah 6:6)

"For unto us a Child is born, unto us a Son is given, and the government will be upon His shoulders. And His name will be called Wonderful, Counselor, Mighty God, Everlasting Father, Prince of Peace. Of the increase of His government and peace there will be no end." (Is 9:6-7)

The one who will occupy the throne of David will have victory over death, as His throne is everlasting and will not be passed on to successors. He will not only be a descendant of David – He will be a direct Son of God.

As students of the scriptures we know that Jesus is the one who fulfills the Davidic Covenant. The angel who spoke to Mary told her that her son *'will be great, and will be called the Son of the Most High; and the Lord will give to him the throne of his father David and he will reign over the house of Jacob forever; and of his kingdom there will be no end."* (Luke 1:32-33*)*

The complete fulfillment of David's Covenant is promised after the Jews have come back to the land of Israel and to Jerusalem. (See Isa. 2) We know from the scriptures that the nations will 'rage' against Israel and Jerusalem (Psalm 2). A false Messiah will bring a false peace, but his rule will come to an end when Jesus returns. (2 Thess. 2:8) His return will fulfill the Davidic Covenant and bring peace from Jerusalem to Israel and the world.

"Now it shall come to pass in the last days that the mountain of the Lord's house shall be established on the top of the mountains, and shall be exalted above the hills and all nations shall flow to it.
Many people shall come and say:
'Come and let us go up to the mountain of the Lord, to the house of the God of Jacob;
He will teach of His ways,
and we shall walk in His paths.'
For out of Zion shall go forth the law,
and the word of the Lord from Jerusalem.
He shall judge between the nations,
and rebuke many people;
They shall beat their swords into plowshares,
and their spears into pruning hooks.
Nation shall not lift up sword against nation,
Neither shall they learn war anymore." (Isaiah 2)

The Davidic Covenant guarantees the restoration of Israel and the rule of the Messiah.

- The *Abrahamic Covenant* promises possession of the Land of Promise to Israel that will bless not just them but all nations.
- The *Sinai Covenant* foreshadows an eternal sacrifice to bear the sins of the world.
- The *New Covenant* brings forgiveness and emancipation from sin through a suffering servant and the impartation of righteousness by God coming to dwell *in* us.
- The *Davidic Covenant* promises a triumphant glorious Ruler who brings in a world order under the rule of His righteousness and peace.

The present flow of history is about to climax in the triumphant coming (return) of the Messiah to fulfill *the Davidic Covenant.* This will be the culmination of all four covenants for Israel and the nations.

When Jesus came the first time He inaugurated the New Covenant and atoned for the sins of the world. Many of the Jewish people failed to recognize Him as the Messiah because He did not at that time fulfill all the promises contained in the Davidic Covenant and assert Himself as the triumphant heir to David's throne ruling from Jerusalem. This is the reason for His Second Coming. *"This same Jesus who was taken up from you into heaven, will so come in like manner as you saw Him go into heaven."* (Acts 1:10) He will return again to occupy the throne of David and to rule the earth from Jerusalem. Then, as the prophet foretold, *"the earth will be filled with the knowledge of the glory of the Lord."* (Habakkuk 2:14)

"Now when you see these things begin to happen, look up, and lift up your heads for your redemption draws nigh." (Lk. 21:28)

The present world order was set in motion when Adam opened a gateway for man's independent and demonically influenced self-rule of the earth to be replaced by the union of heaven and earth by the Messiah. The Davidic Covenant promises the incorruptible rule of the Messiah over all the earth. God's plan is not just a plan for personal salvation but to redeem Israel and all the nations.

Conclusion

Ignoring this covenant has distorted Christian teaching. Traditional Christianity has for the most part not given a coherent vison for the destiny of the planet and many have been led to live without hope. Life on earth without a goal or a vision becomes meaningless and Christianity seemed to offer as its critics put it 'pie in the sky when we die' but no hope for the uplifting and healing of the nations.

Even when Christianity does address the issue of the return of the Lord it does so outside the framework of the Davidic Covenant with its marvelous promises. As a result the focus shifts from the coming golden age of the triumph of the Messiah to the tribulations, "birth pangs" and difficulties that precede it. The focus is often more on the problems that assail the earth rather than on the solution the return of the Lord will bring when He fulfills the Davidic Covenant.

The Davidic Covenant presents a glorious plan and sure promise to lift all nations from oppression and for God's wonderful future for mankind. This plan is inherently connected with the vision of the prophets and the destiny and calling of the Jewish people and the restoration to Jerusalem.

Because of this covenant we know that God has a plan and purposes for world history. Life on earth is not futile. History is being propelled forward by the hidden hand of God to a glorious conclusion and climax. As we glimpse God's extraordinary purposes for the earth and for mankind, we will no longer be tossed to and fro by every wind of political ideology but enter into lives of meaning and vision.

CHAPTER 7

REPLACEMENT THEOLOGY

The New Covenant relates to the Sinai Covenant as prophecy is related to fulfillment. It does not *replace* the Sinai Covenant; it *fulfills* it. The two are related as summer is related to spring. One fulfills what the other anticipates.

'Replacement theology' is the name we give to the false theology that teaches that the Church replaces Israel and that the New Testament replaces all other covenants that God made with the children of Israel. Our study of the covenants shows us that such a position is entirely without ground either from the first thirty-nine books or the last twenty-seven books of the Scriptures.

It is not our purpose to refute Replacement Theology in detail here. It is enough to say that it is totally without foundation in the scriptures, and requires that God be unfaithful to His word, His promises and His covenants.

In spite of this it has been widely accepted among many professing Christians at least since the fifth century. It has become a major source of anti-Semitism in the world and a cause of darkness and lack of blessing in the church. It has provided a theological underpinning for the Spanish Inquisition, the Russian pogroms and the Holocaust in Central Europe. It has furthermore alienated the greater part of the Jewish people from the claims and blessing of the New Covenant.

The New Testament writings themselves declare that the Abrahamic Covenant is eternal and irrevocable. Paul addressed the situation of the Jewish people who do not understand or believe in the new covenant. He writes: *"concerning the gospel they are enemies for your sake, but* concerning the election they are beloved for the sake of the fathers *(i.e. Abraham, Isaac and Jacob.) For the gifts and the calling of*

84

God are irrevocable." (Romans 11:28-29)

The covenant with Israel is not revoked by any failure on their part. Similarly, the Davidic Covenant (through which God promises to set up a righteous eternal Kingdom in Israel is also irreplaceable and irrevocable.

"Thus says the Lord, who gives the sun for a light by day and the ordinances of the moon and the stars for a light by night, who disturbs the sea and its waves roar (The Lord of hosts is His name): 'If those ordinances depart from before Me,' says the Lord then the seed of Israel shall also cease from being a nation before me forever.'... 'If you can break My covenant with the day and My covenant with the night, so that there will not be day and night in their season, then My covenant may also be broken with David My servant so that he shall not have a son to reign on his throne and with the Levites the priests my ministers.'"
(Jeremiah 31: 35-36 & 33:2-21)

God Cannot Lie

To teach replacement theology would require us to believe that God would cancel His word to Abraham and to his descendants, and abandon His promise to David. If replacement theology is true then

- God cannot be trusted,
- the word of God is not to be relied upon and
- the basis of our faith is void.

There is no replacement of the Abrahamic or of the Davidic Covenant by the New Covenant. The Sinai Covenant is fulfilled (but not removed) by the New Covenant. Replacement Theology requires that God does the one thing He cannot do - lie. When God promises something He will fulfill it.

"God is not a man, that He should lie, Nor a son of man, that He should repent. Has He said, and will He not do? Or has He spoken, and will He not make it good?"
(Numbers 23.19)

The Blessings Of Abraham

"Christ redeemed us from the curse of the law by becoming a curse for us -for it is written, "Cursed is everyone who is hanged on a tree" - so that in Christ Jesus the blessing of Abraham might come to the Gentiles, so that we might receive the promised Spirit through faith." (Galatians 3:13-14)

This statement is one of the best-loved summaries of the entire gospel message. Here we learn that Jesus took the curse of the Law upon Himself so that blessings of Abraham might be fulfilled.

The blessings of Abraham *"In you all the families of the earth will be blessed' (Genesis 12:3)* can now come upon the gentiles because in His death Jesus has born the sin and guilt of the world. When the nations put their faith in this reality they can be reconciled with God and receive not only pardon but the Holy Spirit (New birth) and be released from the curse to be blessed with the blessing of Abraham.

If the Covenant with Abraham has ceased to exist how can we receive the blessing promised in that Covenant? If the blessings of Abraham are real and available today then the Abrahamic covenant is in operation today. You cannot believe in the blessings of Abraham without believing in the Abrahamic Covenant! If the part of the Covenant that has to do with the blessings of the Gentiles still stands then the part of the covenant that deals with his blessing of the descendants of

Abraham, Isaac and Jacob must still stand also!

To Confirm The Covenant Of The Fathers

"For I tell you that Christ became a servant to the circumcised to show God's truthfulness, in order to confirm the promises given to the patriarchs, and in order that the Gentiles might glorify God for his mercy." (Romans 15:8)

If there can be any doubt left of the perfect compatibility of the New Covenant with the Abrahamic Covenant Paul's statement should be sufficient to remove all doubt. Here he states that Jesus' became a servant to the Jewish people to confirm God's promises given to them through the patriarchs, Abraham Isaac and Jacob. Thus, the New Covenant and the ministry of Jesus ***confirm*** and do not annul the promises given to the Jewish people.

The Testimony Of Mary

It is evident that Paul saw the ministry of Jesus as confirming the promises given to Abraham and the patriarchs. This is also seen in the gospel of Luke when Mary, the mother of

Jesus, rejoiced in the coming of the Messiah by describing the coming of her Son as God's intervention on behalf of Israel to fulfill His promises to Abraham, Isaac and Jacob.

"He has helped His servant Israel,
in remembrance of his mercy,
as he spoke to our fathers,
to Abraham and to his offspring forever." (Luke 1:54-55)

In the same chapter Zechariah, the father of John the Baptist echoes Mary's words when he prophesies and describes the coming of Jesus as a fulfillment of the Covenant with Abraham.

"Blessed be the Lord God of Israel for He has visited and redeemed His people. He has raised up a horn (leader) of salvation for us in the house of His servant David as He spoke by the mouth of His holy prophets ... to show the mercy promised to our fathers, to remember His holy covenant, the oath he swore to our father Abraham" (Luke 1:68-69; 72-73)

The failure of Christianity to acknowledge this essential part of its message has had tragic consequences for Christianity and for the Jewish history. As a consequence, the Jewish people have been marginalized, expelled, forced to convert, tortured as heretics, confined to ghettos, murdered in programs, and finally virtually annihilated in 20th century Germany at the hands of those educated in Christian churches and schools.

Even today their rerun to the land of promise is undermined and opposed by millions of Christian worldwide. We cannot afford to allow this heresy of replacement theology to continue within Christianity.

What a wonderful recovery will take place when believers in Yeshua see His ministry in the context of the Abrahamic and Davidic Covenants as Mary, Elizabeth, Zechariah and Luke did.

CHAPTER 8

CONSEQUENCES

The understanding of these four great covenants is a key to interpreting the scriptures and understanding the plan of God for redemption.

What Difference Does It Make?

1) Because the Church failed to understand the permanence of the Abrahamic Covenant it fell into anti-Semitism and created a misunderstanding of the relationship between Christians and Jews. These misunderstandings had appalling consequences for the Jewish people worldwide. Professing Christians through the

centuries have participated in atrocities against the Jewish people and became conspirators and facilitators of those who hate and oppose God's plan for Israel and the Jews.

To this day, while the church repents of anti-Semitism and being, ignorant of the Abrahamic Covenant, is often anti-Zionist. They fail to recognize that to be Anti-Zionist (i.e. anti the settling of the Jewish people in the land covenanted to them by God) is to be anti-Semitic as it opposes the Jewish people fulfilling their God given destiny.

Some consider Zionism to be a form of racism. While there may be a few racist Zionists, Biblical Zionism is simply the standing in faith with God's plan to bring Israel back to its land in remembrance of His covenant with Abraham. Since the call on Abraham is to bring blessing to the whole world, true Zionism is the opposite of racism as it is a divine plan to bring blessing not only to Israel but also to **every** nation and ethnic group.

Millions of Christians ignore the call of God on the Jewish people and fail to pray for the return of Israel to their land. This has resulted in professing Christians actually opposing the settlement of Jewish people in their own land and allying with political movements that are directly opposed to God's plans as revealed in the Abrahamic Covenant.

2) Failure to understand the Sinai covenant has resulted in millions of professing believers living without a sense of moral accountability and casting off restraint.

3) Failure to understand the New Covenant has resulted in millions of believers living in condemnation, legalism and powerlessness. This ignorance has also alienated Jewish people from the gospel. The New Covenant as we have seen is continuous with the plan of God in the Old Testament. Jesus did not form a new religion but led His people and as many as would join with Him on to further and fuller dimension in God.

4) Finally failure to understand the Abrahamic Covenant has caused countless believers to live in ignorance of God's plan for the redemption of the earth.

Even today in many churches the return of

the Lord is taught as a plan of God to remove His people from the earth rather than as His plan to redeem and restore the earth. "*For the earth shall be full of the knowledge of the Lord, as the waters cover the sea.*" (Isaiah 11:9)

We have been given a faulty focus. We have focused primarily on 'getting to heaven' instead of working with God to bring more and more of heaven's rule to earth.

It is hoped that the understanding of the covenants presented in this book will help the church to recover a greater understanding of the plan of God, and the gospel of the kingdom as understood by Jesus and His first followers.

CHAPTER 9

DAVID'S TABERNACLE & THE NEW TESTAMENT

The apostles used two prophecies to summarize the activity of God in the book of Acts: -

(1) Joel's prophecy of an outpouring of the Spirit on all flesh (Joel 2:28-32 & Acts 2:17-21)

(2) Amos's prophecy of the restoration of David's Tabernacle. (Amos Chapter 9:11-12 & Acts 15:16-18)

While Peter described the events of the Book of Acts as the 'outpouring of the Spirit on all flesh' foretold by Joel; James described the events of the Book of Acts as 'the restoration of David's Tabernacle' foretold by Amos. So, according to the apostles, the New Testament era is the era of the restoration of David's Tabernacle – the era beyond the Law and of the proclamation of the kingdom of God to every nation.

Much attention is given to how the work of the Holy Spirit fulfills Joel's prophecy but little attention has been given, until now, to how His work also fulfills Amos' prophecy.

The Council At Jerusalem

Acts Chapter 15 reports that the apostles and elders of the early church - the messianic community - gathered in Jerusalem to discuss how gentiles responding to the gospel were to be treated. These gentiles (mainly from the Roman and Greek communities) were

- being touched by the miraculous power of God's kingdom,
- believing in the atoning work of Yeshua,
- receiving the Holy Spirit
- and being added to the church.

For the first time the Jewish leaders of the church had to deal with the inclusion of gentiles into the household of faith. Should they be required to become Jews, observe the laws of Moses and be circumcised or should different criteria be adopted?

"The apostles and the elders were gathered together to consider this matter. And after there had been much debate, Peter stood up and said to them, "Brothers, you know that in the early days God made a choice among you, that by my mouth the Gentiles should hear the word of the gospel and believe. And God, who knows the heart, bore witness to them, by giving them the Holy Spirit just as he did to us, and he made no distinction between them and us having cleansed their hearts by faith. Now, therefore, why are you putting God to the test by placing a yoke on the neck of the disciples that neither our fathers nor we have been able to bear? But we believe that we will be saved through the grace of the Lord Yeshua, just as they will."

"And all the assembly fell silent, and they listened to Barnabas and Paul as they related what signs and wonders God had done through them among the Gentiles. After they finished speaking, James replied, "Brothers, listen to me. Simeon has related how God first visited the Gentiles, to take from them a people for his name. And with this the words of the prophets agree, just as it is written, "'After this I will return, and I will rebuild the tent of David that has fallen; I will rebuild its ruins, and I will restore it, that the rest of mankind may seek the Lord, and all the Gentiles who

are called by my name, says the Lord, who makes these
things known from of old.' Therefore my judgment is that we
should not trouble those of the Gentiles who turn to God, but
should write to them to abstain from the things polluted by
idols, and from sexual immorality, and from what has been
strangled, and from blood. For from ancient generations
Moses has had in every city those who proclaim him, for he
is read every Sabbath in the synagogues." (Acts 15:6-15)

James described the inclusion of Gentiles
along with Jews into the household of faith
(through faith in the finished work of Yeshua) as
the 'restoration of David's Tabernacle'. If the
work of the Holy Spirit in the book of Acts is
described as the restoration of the Tabernacle of
David we need to know

(1)   What is David's Tabernacle?

(2)   What did James describe as the 'restoration
of David's Tabernacle"?

What is David's Tabernacle?

When David became King of Israel and
established Jerusalem as the capital of the
Kingdom he decided to bring the Ark of the
Covenant into Jerusalem. (The Ark had been

captured by the Philistines and eventually returned to Israel where it had remained for several years in the house of Obed Edom.) (1 Chron. 15:25 –16:2)

David could have returned the Ark to its place in the Holy of Holies of Moses' Tabernacle but instead he decided to prepare a totally new tent (tabernacle) for it in Jerusalem. This new Tabernacle, which David erected in Jerusalem, is known as the Tabernacle of David. It was not simply a temporary tent until the Temple was built. It was a completely *different* tent from the tent that Moses had built for the Ark of the Covenant and represented a new way of approaching God.

Moses' Tabernacle Contrasted To David's Tabernacle

At Sinai God had given Moses elaborate details about the construction and rituals of the Tabernacle. At Moses' Tabernacle there were three partitions: The Outer Court, The Inner Court and The Holy of Holies. The central object of the Tabernacle was The Ark Of The Covenant, which was symbolic of the Mercy of God, the

Presence of God and the Rule of God. The Ark, concealed in the Holy of Holies, could only be approached through the outer court and inner court and then only by the High Priest once a year.

The new tent, "The Tabernacle of David", which David erected for the Ark in Jerusalem abandoned the protocols of Moses' Tabernacle. This was not simply a relaxation of protocol. It was a revolution! It prophetically anticipates the days of the Messiah Yeshua who replaced the repeated sacrifices of Moses' Tabernacle with the once-for-all sacrifice at Calvary in Jerusalem.

While the Tabernacle of Moses was a place of repeated sacrifices each morning and each evening, The Tabernacle of David was based on the concept of completed sacrifice. This is why it anticipates THE NEW ORDER established after the complete sacrifice of Yeshua on the cross. When David brought the Ark to Jerusalem he made a temporary end of the sacrifices as a prophetic foretaste of the era when the repeated sacrifices of Moses' Tabernacle would no longer be necessary having been replaced by the once-for-all Sacrifice of Yeshua.

"And when David had **finished** *offering the burnt offerings and the peace offerings, he blessed the people in the name of the Lord and distributed to all Israel, both men and women, to each a loaf of bread, a portion of wine and a cake of raisins."* (1 Chronicles 16.2)

David finished the sacrifices. After that no more sacrifices were offered at David's Tabernacle only sacrifices of praise and thanksgiving. Like David, The Messiah, Yeshua, distributed bread and wine. He gave the bread and wine as the means of commemorating and activating the benefits of His once for all sacrifice for the sins of the world. No more sacrifice is necessary except the sacrifice of praise and thanksgiving for what He has already done.

Jesus, one thousand years after David, from the Cross He declared: *"It is finished"* and as He did the veil of the Temple was rent in two from top to bottom. Thus He created a tent without a veil so that all men could approach the mercy of God as in the days of David. This is why the apostles described the days following the death, resurrection, and ascension of Yeshua as the restoration of David's Tabernacle. We are now in a whole new era of access to God and His blessing for Jew and gentile through the finished sacrifice of Jesus.

The Tabernacle of Moses was an arrangement providing temporary atonement until the final sacrifice is made. The Tabernacle of David was a foretaste of the day of completed sacrifice, completed reconciliation and perfect access to the blessing for Jew and gentile together on the basis of the completed sacrifice of Yeshua. (He fulfilled exactly the type and shadow of Moses' Tabernacle. He is the Door; the Sacrifice; the Laver; the Light of the world; the Bread of Life and He are Glory of The Father reigning from the Throne of Grace.)

"And every priest stands daily at his service, offering repeatedly the same sacrifices, which can never take away sins. But when Christ had offered for all time a single sacrifice for sins, he sat down at the right hand of God, waiting from that time until his enemies should be made a footstool for his feet. For by a single offering he has perfected for all time those who are being sanctified. (Hebrews 10:11-14)

The sacrifices of Moses' Tabernacle are replaced by the perfect sacrifice, which can perfect for all time those who are being sanctified. The Tabernacle of David therefore represents a realm where there is no more guilt no more separation, no more fear to draw near to God, no more sin consciousness, no more priesthood class standing between us and God. It is the realm where the blood of Yeshua takes all who will believe into the grace and blessing of God.

Summary Of The Differences Between The Two Tabernacles

- *Moses' Tabernacle was based on repeated sacrifices;*
- *David's Tabernacle is based on* **one** *perfect Sacrifice.*
- *While Moses Tabernacle had three partitions,*
- *David's Tabernacle had no partitions.*
- *Only priests could enter the Tabernacle of Moses*
- *All Israelis from every tribe could enter David's Tabernacle.*
- *Only men could enter The Tabernacle of Moses.*
- *Women could also enter David's Tabernacle.*

- *Only Israelis could approach the ark at Moses Tabernacle.*
- *Even Gentile could approach the ark at David Tabernacle.*
- *The Blessings of Moses' Tabernacle were restricted to Jewish people.*
- *The blessings of David's Tabernacle were available to all.*
- *Moses' Tabernacle was mediated by a succession of priests.*
- *David's Tabernacle is mediated and fulfilled by one eternal Perfect Priest, Yeshua.*
- *Moses' Tabernacle brings guilt consciousness*
- *David's Tabernacle brings son consciousness.*
- *Moses Tabernacle was a place without music*
- *David's Tabernacle was a place of singing, musical instruments, dancing and celebration.*
- *Moses' Tabernacle was given at Sinai.*
- *David's Tabernacle was given in Jerusalem (Zion).*

Though David did not worship at Moses' Tabernacle, he did not dishonor it. *"He left Zadok the priest and his brothers .. before the Tabernacle of the Lord in the high place at Gibeon"* (I Chron. 16:39) but the glory of God represented by the ark was not in

Gibeon but in the Tent in Jerusalem

Characteristics Of David's Tabernacle

"So all Israel brought up the Ark of the covenant of the Lord with shouting, to the sound of the horn, trumpets, and cymbals, and made loud music on harps and lyres. And as the Ark of the Covenant of the Lord came to the city of David, Michal the daughter of Saul looked out of the window and saw King David dancing and rejoicing, and she despised him in her heart." (2 Samuel 6:15-16)

"And they brought in the Ark of God and set it inside the tent that David had pitched for it, and they offered burnt offerings and peace offerings before God. And when David had finished offering the burnt offerings and the peace offerings, he blessed the people in the name of the Lord and distributed to all Israel, both men and women, to each a loaf of bread, a portion of 'wine' and a cake of raisins. Then he appointed some of the Levites as ministers before the Ark of the Lord, to invoke, to thank, and to praise the Lord, the God of Israel." (I Chronicles 16:1-4 Young's Literal Trans.)

David's Song of Thanks

"Oh give thanks to the Lord; call upon his name; make

105

known his deeds among the peoples! Sing to him; sing praises to him; tell of all his wondrous works! Glory in his holy name; let the hearts of those who seek the Lord rejoice! Seek the Lord and his strength; seek his presence continually! Remember the wondrous works that he has done, his miracles and the judgments he uttered!..
Remember his covenant forever, the word he commanded, for a thousand generations, the covenant that he made with Abraham, his sworn promise to Isaac, which he confirmed as a statute to Jacob, as an everlasting covenant to Israel, saying, "To you I will give the land of Canaan, as your portion for an inheritance."..... Let the heavens be glad, and the earth rejoice, and let them say among the nations, "The Lord reigns!" His steadfast love endures forever!"
(1 Chron. 16: 8 - 36)

More Characteristics Of David's Tabernacle

We have seen that according to I Chronicles 16 David's Tabernacle was a place of celebration, reconciliation and blessing. It was a place where Jew and gentile, male and female could approach the throne of God (symbolized and conveyed by the ark) and receive the blessing of God on their lives. It was a place where people worshipped with music, dancing, shouts and praises, remembered God's miraculous power and sought His strength.

This was a foretaste of the release of glory that followed Yeshua' ascension! As He was leaving He explained to His disciples that He had provided permanent atonement for the sins of the world as the Isaiah, Jeremiah and John had predicted. He charged them to proclaim this good news to Israel and the nations.

But before they went to announce reconciliation and forgiveness of sins based on His work on the cross they were to wait until they were *"clothed with power from on high."* They were, as David had said, "to seek the Lord and his strength" and *"remember His marvelous works"*. They were to seek and receive the power of the Holy Spirit to walk in the ways that Yeshua had taught them and to do the miracles He had demonstrated. (John 14:12; Mark 16:17)

What Did James Describe As The Restoration of David's Tabernacle?

In Acts chapter 15 we read that the disciples met together in Jerusalem to consider their response to the outpouring of the Holy Spirit and the operation of miraculous sings and wonders among the gentiles as well as on the Jewish community. There James remembered Amos' prophecy of the restoration of David's Tabernacle where Jew and Gentile, male and female, rejoiced together in the presence of the Lord.

Writing about 250 years after King David, Amos had reminded Israel of the kind of worship that was experienced in Jerusalem in the days of David when Israelis and gentiles came together to celebrate the mercy of God on the basis of the completed sacrifice. Amos foretold that God would restore this kind of worship again.

"In that day I will raise up the booth of David that is fallen and repair its breaches, and raise up its ruins and rebuild it as in the days of old" (Amos 9:11)

As James recalled Amos' prophecy he

concluded that the events and the outpouring of the Spirit on Jews and gentiles after the death, resurrection and ascension of Yeshua was the fulfillment of Amos' prophecy. The joy and celebration in Jerusalem in the days after the Pentecost outpouring of the Holy Spirit resembled the joy that had been in Jerusalem in the days of David's Tabernacle.

The apostles did not imitate David by *literally* erecting a tent in Jerusalem. They recognized that Yeshua's death had torn the veil separating mankind from the Holy of Holies and opening up access for all believers to the throne of God. The rending of the veil (that had separated man from the Mercy of God) by the death of Yeshua on the Cross made His mercy available to all believers everywhere and brings Jew and gentile together in His presence. *"For he himself is our peace, who has made us both one and has broken down in his flesh the dividing wall of hostility by abolishing the law of commandments expressed in ordinances, that he might create in himself one new man in place of the two, so making peace, and might reconcile us both to God in one body through the cross, thereby killing the hostility. And he came and preached peace to you who were far off and peace to those who were near. For through him we both have access in one Spirit to the Father."* (Ephes. 2:14-18)

The Apostles' Conclusion

The Apostles concluded that Gentiles who were coming to faith in Yeshua and were receiving the Holy Spirit and the blessing of God on their lives did not have to become Jews or adopt Jewish culture.

Peter stood up and said to them, *"Brothers, you know that in the early days God made a choice among you, that by my mouth the Gentiles should hear the word of the gospel and believe. And God, who knows the heart, bore witness to them, by giving them the Holy Spirit just as he did to us, and he made no distinction between them, and us having cleansed their hearts by faith. "Now, therefore, why are you putting God to the test by placing a yoke on the neck of the disciples that neither our fathers nor we have been able to bear? But we believe that we will be saved through the grace of the Lord Yeshua, just as they will. "* (Acts 15:7-11)

James agreed saying: *"Therefore my judgment is that we should not trouble those of the Gentiles who turn to God, but should write to them to abstain from the things polluted by idols, and from sexual immorality, and from what has been strangled, and from blood."* (Acts 15:19-20)

The culture of Judaism and Jewish ritual should not be imposed upon them. They were however required to abandon any form of idolatry and sexual immorality from their previous life and pagan culture. The message of the Council of Jerusalem is neatly summed up in the Book of Galatians where Paul explains:

"Christ redeemed us from the curse of the law by becoming a curse for us for it is written, 'Cursed is everyone who is hanged on a tree' so that in Christ Yeshua the blessing of Abraham might come to the Gentiles, so that we might receive the promised Spirit through faith." (Galatians 3:13-14)

The consequence of receiving the Holy Spirit is that we enter into a loving relationship with God and receive a pure heart from which develop the fruit of the spirit. Gentiles were not placed under the observances of the Jewish law, but were simply required to remove all immorality from their lives, especially sexual immorality and

111

idolatry. The gift of the Spirit replaces the sinful part of our nature with the life of God. Idolatry, sexual immorality and other sins, contrary to the fruit of the spirit are therefore opposed to the Spirit-filled life. *"But the fruit of the Spirit is love, joy, peace, patience, kindness, goodness, faithfulness, gentleness, self-control; against such things there is no law."* (Gal. 5:22-23)

The Consequences of the Apostles Ruling

Abraham had received a preview of the gospel when God said to him *"in you ALL the families of the earth shall be blessed."* (Genesis 12:3) He saw the day when the fount of blessing that had been received by His family would extend to all nations.

At the meeting at Jerusalem the apostles recognized that the atonement of Yeshua had provided perfect access for all to the grace and blessing of God, and that this access was not on the basis of Jewish ritual or even the law of Moses. The revolution here is that the apostles and evangelists could go in to the world not to co-opt people to the Jewish religion (which, according to Peter, the Jews themselves had not observed very well [Acts 15:11 op. cit.]) but to proclaim the redemption of

112

God to Jews and gentiles everywhere on the basis of the sacrifice of Yeshua.

They were not required to export a religion or a culture but to spread a message: the good news of the Kingdom of God. The gospel of the Kingdom was released from any form of cultural or religious colonialism. The message was not: "Join our religion." but *"Be reconciled to God."*

The gentiles would not have to abandon their ethnic culture but simply the idolatry and immorality that had become embedded in their culture. Thus Christianity is not a matter of cultural domination but simply the reconciling of all to God on the basis of Yeshua' work. The Jew remains a Jew with his unique call, talents and gifts and the foreigner remains a foreigner with his unique gifts and calling. The foreigner however, while still ethnically and culturally different is no longer a stranger or enemy. The hostility between Jew and gentile is broken. They are no longer strangers but brothers in the grace of God each equally enjoying His mercy and blessing on their lives through Yeshua.

"So then you are no longer strangers and aliens, but you

are fellow citizens with the saints and members of the household of God." (Ephesians 2:19)

Idolatry & Sexual Immorality Prohibited

The apostles laid no ritual requirement on the gentile believers but they did not weaken the moral law and especially, as we have seen, required repentance from sexual immorality and idolatry.

These may seem very simple requirements and yet today in the church throughout the world we find that many believers have not renounced and put away idolatry and/or sexual immorality. Because these sins are so prevalent today, pastors and church leaders are often fearful of addressing these subjects lest they lose too many church members! Today sexual immorality is considered normal and regarded by the world the natural expression of the gift of sex. However, the scriptures teach that any sexual intercourse outside of marriage is sexual immorality and the use of pornography and other sexual fantasy is adultery of the heart.

Idolatry also is still prevalent today not only where people worship other gods and worship saints as if gods. It is also present in free masonry; secret occult practices; divination; witchcraft; necromancy or communication with the dead; in occult magic and other para-psychic activity all of which are common today. According to the apostles' directive in Jerusalem, we must put off such practices if we are to maintain a relationship with God and His blessings and walk in the anointing and power of the Holy Spirit.

Most believers today are coming from a past where sexual sins and idolatry of some sort had impacted their lives. God through Yeshua forgives and cleanses but then He empowers us to sin no more as He gives us a new heart and a new spirit that empowers us to avoid these life-destroying sins and to live in the dignity of sons and daughters of God. None of us should be finger pointes but we should help one another to develop the habits and lifestyle of the kingdom of God and to turn away from and receive cleansing and forgiveness from sexual sin and idolatry.

All of this is part of the restoration of the

Tabernacle of David as foretold by Amos and interpreted by the apostles. (Amos 9:11 Acts 15:16 -29)

CHAPTER 10

DAVID'S TABERNACLE RESTORED AGAIN TODAY

The Restoration of Israel

"In that day I will raise up the booth of David that is fallen and repair its breaches, and raise up its ruins and rebuild it as in the days of old, that they may possess the remnant of Edom and all the nations who are called by my name," declares the Lord who does this.

"Behold, the days are coming," declares the Lord, *when the plowman shall overtake the reaper and the trader of grapes him who sows the seed; the mountains shall drip sweet wine, and all the hills shall flow with it. I will restore the fortunes of my people Israel, and they shall rebuild the ruined cities and inhabit them; they shall plant vineyards*

117

and drink their wine, and they shall make gardens and eat their fruit I will plant them on their land, and they shall never again be uprooted out of the land that I have given them, " says the Lord your God.' (Amos 9:1-15)

James quoted Amos 9:11 but he did not quote the rest of the passage. He recognized that Amos 9:11 described the situation of the first century church where Jew and gentile are one before the throne of God experiencing His mercy and the demonstration of the power of God . The rest of the passage describes a move of God that is to take place in the twentieth and twenty first century (see below). It is an extraordinary passage that predicts a further restoration of David's Tabernacle in our day.

Amos speaks of this restoration of David's Tabernacle at a time when the Jews will come back to Israel from all the nations never to be uprooted. This return to Israel is described as been accompanied by fruit farming and especially the planting of the vine and drinking the wine. (Amos 9:14) This reference to wine contains a hidden time reference that we now know refers to the twentieth and twenty first centuries and predicts a

118

new restoration of David's Tabernacle in our day!

In the middle of the seventh century Israel came under Islamic rule. From that time Israel remained under Islamic rule until 1917 (except for a short period of 88 years when it was ruled by the Crusaders (1099-1187)

Under Moslem rule it was illegal (as it is today in Islamic counties) to grow the grape vine or to sell fermented grapes. By describing the cultivation of the vine and the drinking of wine on the mountains of Israel the prophecy is clearly predicting a day when Islamic rule would come to an end in Israel. This happened in 1917 and since then the vine has been cultivated in Israel. The growing of the vine in Amos' prophecy is therefore a hidden time reference stating that when Israel comes back to the land and Muslim rules ends over the Holy Land, God will once again restore the Tabernacle of David. Amos' prophecy therefore refers to the restoration of David's Tabernacle in our days.

God is saying that three events will take place simultaneously

(1)   The restoration of Israel and

119

(2)   The end of Muslim rule over the holy land

(3)   And further restoration of the Tabernacle of David

Simultaneous to the end of Muslim rule over Israel and Israel's return to their land there will be a release of the activity of the Spirit that was evident in the book of Acts (which as we have seen James describes as the restoration of the Tabernacle of David.) This supernatural element of Christianity will be restored, the Jew and gentile will be reconciled in the Messiah and the gospel will adapt to every culture. Mission will no longer be a matter of colonization but of the outpouring of the Holy Spirit and all nations discovering the blessings that are available to them through the work of Yeshua. The gospel of the kingdom will be preached in every nation and the Jewish people will return to the Lord in ways that parallel the first century.

There is nothing anti-Arab in the proclamation that the end of Muslim rule is part of the final restoration of David's Tabernacle. The restored David's Tabernacle will release the blessing of God not only on the Jewish and Christian people but on all people (including Arabs) who draw close to God to receive the blessings made available to although the Atoning work of Yeshua.

God promised to bless Abraham's descendants through Isaac and Jacob, but He also promised to extend His mercies to all nations. The final restoration of David's Tabernacle that coincides with the end of Muslim rule over the Holy Land will release God's blessing on the Arab people. The people who so long have felt rejected and estranged from god's covenants will also find the means of reconciliation with God through the revelation of the Atoning sacrifice of Yeshua.

This is exactly what is happening today. Israel has come back; the rue of Islam has been replaced in much of the ancient land and the power of the Holy Spirit is being experienced in the church among the nations like never before since the book of acts. The restoration of supernatural power of the Book of Acts and the restoration of Israel are two sides of a simultaneous move of God that will continue until the return of the Lord prophesied by David.

Characteristics Of The Restoration Of The Tabernacle of David

The present restoration of Israel and the end of Muslim rule over the land of Israel is no accident of history. James, as we have seen, described the inclusion of Gentiles along with Jews as the fulfillment of Amos' prophecy of the restoration of David's Tabernacle. When he said this, he was responding to the report brought by Paul and Barnabas of *"how many miracles and wonders God had worked through them among the Gentiles."* (Acts 15:12)

If the events of the Book of Acts are described as 'the restoration of David's Tabernacle. The present day restoration of Israel to their land should coincide with and trigger events similar to the Book of Acts. This is what we see today.

- The rise of indigenous Christianity in every nation is no accident of history.
- The restoration of the Pentecostal power of the Book of Acts to the true church

• The recognition by Jews today of Yeshua as the Messiah without having to compromise their Jewish identity is no accident of history.

• All of these are foreseen in the prophecy of Amos and all of these are being experienced today. We are living in days foretold by the prophets and in dimensions of restoration that are reserved for our time.

• It is a matter of historical fact that the demonstration of supernatural power of God waned from the church as early as the second century coinciding with the establishment of Gentile control over the land of Israel. So great was this loss of power that some theologians began to come up with the opinion that the gifts and the supernatural anointings of the book of Acts were only for the early church. This teaching known as *'cessationism'* paralleled the other mistaken opinion of many Christian teachers that God was finished with Israel. This teaching is known as *'replacement theology'*.

The prophecy of Amos speaks of a day - our day - when God will by His work and intervention disprove these two mistaken opinions by restoring

Israel and restoring the supernatural power of the Spirit to the church. The church that is flowing with God's present day work will abandon these assumptions and work in solidarity with God's purposes for Israel and His purpose to bless all nations through His redemptive work in fulfillment of the covenant with Abraham. They will also recognize that they cannot serve Him without embracing the supernatural gifts, including signs, wonders, miracles, healings and the baptism in the Holy Spirit that propelled the early church to 'turn the world upside down' with the good news of the kingdom.

Are you embracing His plan and the special dimension of grace that He has reserved for this privileged era of the completed restoration of the Tabernacle of David?

CONCLUSION

For centuries the Body of Christ has neglected and ignored the truth about these great covenants.

We forgot the words of Paul:

"Therefore remember that you, once Gentiles in the flesh - who are called Uncircumcision by what is called the Circumcision made in the flesh by hands— that at that time you were without Christ, being aliens from the commonwealth of Israel and strangers from the covenants of promise, having no hope and without God in the world. But now in Christ Jesus you who once were far off have been brought near by the blood of Christ.

···· Now, therefore, you are no longer strangers and foreigners, but fellow citizens with the saints and members of the household of God, having been built on the foundation of the apostles and prophets, Jesus Christ Himself being the chief cornerstone, in whom the whole building, being fitted

together, grows into a holy temple in the Lord, in whom you also are being built together for a dwelling place of God in the Spirit." (Ephesians 2: 11-13, 19-22)

The invitation to be "strangers no longer" to God's covenants of blessing and be reconciled to God and His people is being released in a new way upon the earth.

About The Authors

PAUL & NUALA O'HIGGINS

Paul & Nuala O'Higgins are the directors of Reconciliation Outreach. They are natives of Ireland now living in Stuart, Florida. They travel extensively throughout the U.S. and Europe in an international ministry of teaching and reconciliation.

Paul holds a doctorate in Biblical theology. They are the authors of several books including *"Christianity Without Religion", "The Tree Of Life"* *"The Feasts Of The Lord"* and *"In Israel Today With Jesus"*

Paul & Nuala O'Higgins,
P.O. Box 2778, Stuart, Florida 34995
USA. Tel. 772-283-6920
paulandnuala@comcast.net
128

Other Books By Paul & Nuala O'Higgins

- Christianity Without Religion
- In Israel Today With Jesus
- Good News In Israel's Feasts
- The Double Gift Of The Holy Spirit
- The Tree Of Life
- The Supernatural   Habits   Of   The   Spirit Empowered Believer
- Life Changing Prayer World Changing,
- The Blessed Hope
- The Beatitudes

For more copies of
"God's Covenants For Today"
write:
Reconciliation Outreach
P.O. Box 2778, Stuart, FL 34995 USA

or go to **www.reconciliationoutreach.net**

God's Covenants For Today

God's Covenants For Today

Printed in Great Britain
by Amazon

79741641R00078